W9-BXL-576

CRAYOLA
ART OF
CODING

A CELEBRATION OF CREATIVE MINDSETS

KIKI PROTTSMAN

Lerner Publications ◆ Minneapolis

To those who are willing to try something new. You are the thinkers and the innovators who keep us moving forward. Thank you.

Official Licensed Product
Lerner Publications Company
An imprint of Lerner Publishing Group, Inc.
241 First Avenue North
Minneapolis, MN 55401 USA

For reading levels and more information, look up this title at www.lernerbooks.com.

Main body text set in ITC Cachet.
Typeface provided by Monotype.

Editor: Andrea Nelson

Library of Congress Cataloging-in-Publication Data

Names: Prottsman, Kiki, author.
Title: Crayola art of coding : a celebration of creative mindsets / Kiki Prottsman.
Description: Minneapolis, MN : Lerner Publications, 2021. | Includes bibliographical references and index. | Audience: Ages 8–12 | Audience: Grades 4–6 | Summary: "Crayola Art of Coding explores the basics of coding, such as sequencing and debugging, using unplugged activities that empower readers to think like coders"— Provided by publisher.
Identifiers: LCCN 2020009961 (print) | LCCN 2020009962 (ebook) | ISBN 9781728403236 (library binding) | ISBN 9781728418568 (ebook)
Subjects: LCSH: Computer programming—Juvenile literature. | Coding theory—Juvenile literature.
Classification: LCC QA76.6115 .P755 2021 (print) | LCC QA76.6115 (ebook) | DDC 005.13—dc23

LC record available at https://lccn.loc.gov/2020009961
LC ebook record available at https://lccn.loc.gov/2020009962

Manufactured in the United States of America
1-48294-48838-8/17/2020

TABLE OF CONTENTS

Think like a Coder

Did you know that coders were around long before computers were invented? It's true! For thousands of years, humans have recorded their lives, dreams, and stories in ways that are easy to save and share. Modern coders explore the world, create amazing entertainment experiences, and even predict the future.

This cave painting in Utah shows icons drawn by someone who lived many years ago. What story do you think is being told?

While not everyone will become a professional coder, learning to think like a coder can help anyone be a better problem solver. When you think like a coder, you look at challenges differently, and you're able to figure out solutions by paying attention to the feedback that you get when things go wrong.

Thinking like a coder can help you navigate anything—from projects at school to getting to the next level in your video game!

Programming and Visual Expression

Coding, sometimes called programming, is the art of creating instructions that a computer can follow. That's an important skill, because computers are everywhere. You probably already know about desktop and laptop computers.

But cell phones, tablets, and other devices are computers too. Even modern alarm clocks, refrigerators, and TVs follow coded instructions.

Think like Ada Lovelace

One hundred years before computers existed, Ada Lovelace dreamed about machines that could solve problems or make music. In 1834 she worked with Charles Babbage on a design for the first programmable mechanical calculator. Lovelace knew that she needed to represent her thoughts in ways the machine could understand. Even though the machine was never built, Lovelace imagined how it would have worked. That's how she became the world's first coder!

One of the first computers used physical instructions to create patterns. Jacquard looms wove different fabrics by reading paper cards encoded with holes that acted like computer programs. Even though a Jacquard loom didn't have a monitor and keyboard as a modern computer has, it was able to read encoded instructions to complete a task. The loom and its paper cards are examples of using code for visual expression—something that humans have been doing for a very long time.

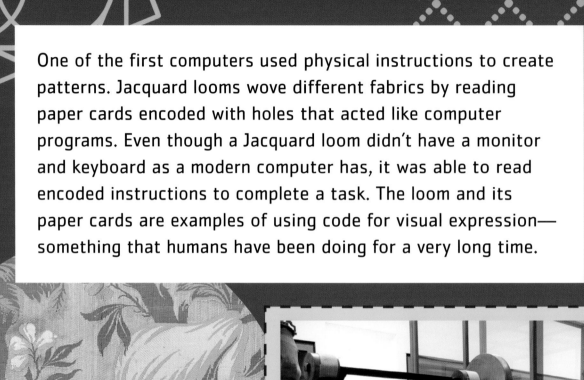

The Jacquard loom (*right*) made it much easier to manufacture woven fabrics with complicated patterns, such as brocade (*above*).

TRY IT!

Pretend you are drawing with a single crayon. Your friend gives you instructions that tell you what to draw. She gives you a paper card with holes in it. What design do you think the code is telling you to make? Why that design and not the others?

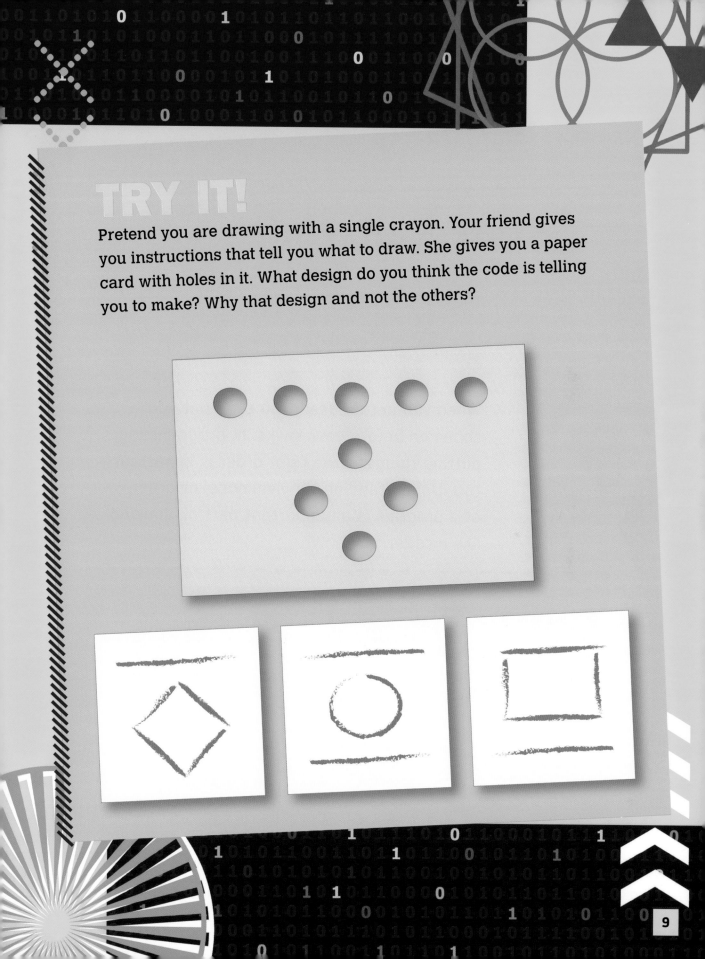

Start, Fail, Finish

When you get dressed, you can't put your shoes on before your socks. In programming, putting things in the right order is important too. Understanding the sequence, or order, of a program is an important part of thinking like a coder.

SEQUENCE

When does order matter in your life? Can you think of something that can happen in any order? What about something that needs to be done in a certain sequence?

For example, it doesn't matter if you put your socks in the washing machine first, then your pants, and then your shirts. They all get clean! But you need to wash your clothes, dry them, and fold them in that order. If you fold them, dry them, and then wash them, you'll be wearing soaked pajamas to bed!

STEP-BY-STEP

Break big jobs down into little tasks to make them feel easier. Cleaning your room might feel like a big job if you don't break it down. Write a list of chores like making your bed, doing your laundry, and picking up toys. Then each task will feel a little easier.

Clean your room! -♡- Mom

BUGS

Sometimes coders make mistakes, but mistakes are great ways to learn! A mistake in code is called a bug. When coders fix bugs, it's called debugging. You can debug other things too! When you've put on your shirt and notice there's an extra buttonhole at the top, you need to find the button you missed and button it. That's debugging.

TRIAL AND ERROR

When you don't know the right way to do something, try the first thing that comes to mind and see what happens. If it goes wrong, make a change to improve your method. Keep trying until you've reached your goal. If you were trying to build a house of cards and it fell, you would look for errors in your design and fix each error as you found it. Eventually you would have a successful design!

SYMBOLS

Many pieces of code look like long strings of words. But code can look like other things too. You can express instructions using simple images or symbols, like emojis! Can you tell what game these images represent?

You can turn anything into code as long as you have a set of rules for what it means. Not everyone has to understand the code you write. As long as it's readable to the person or machine it was intended for, it is doing its job.

Think like Alan Turing

Alan Turing was a famous British computer scientist and a great codebreaker. During World War II (1939–1945), he created a codebreaking machine that saved thousands of Allied lives by decoding German messages. Breaking coded messages that changed every day was hard work, and Turing believed he could build a machine that could do the job. He took inspiration from the calculator developed by Babbage and Lovelace a century earlier. After six months of risk-taking and failing over and over, Turing finished his codebreaker, the British Bombe.

RISK-TAKING

It can be scary to try something if you don't know that you'll get it right. Taking risks is all about being brave enough to do something, even if it takes a few times to succeed.

We're Better Together

Collaborating, or working together with other people, can help you solve problems better and more quickly than you could alone. When you collaborate, you have someone who can offer help when you get stuck or give suggestions for how to improve an idea.

Many teams have changed coding and computers in amazing ways. Bill Gates and Paul Allen started Microsoft together, and Melanie Perkins, Cliff Obrecht, and Cameron Adams teamed up to create Canva, a popular graphic design platform.

Left to right: Cameron Adams, Cliff Obrecht, and Melanie Perkins lead a team of over one thousand people, including developers, designers, engineers, and data specialists.

TRY IT!

Grab a friend, and come up with your own coding language. Imagine you are trying to code someone's movements. What symbols would you use for moving forward or backward? Right or left? What symbol could you use for stop? Use the language to code instructions for a treasure hunt!

- Grab two sheets of paper.
- Fold each sheet in half four times to get two grids of sixteen blocks.
- On one sheet of paper, lightly draw a star in one of the blocks. This is your treasure. In a block on the other sheet, write "start."
- Get a third sheet of paper and use your new language to write directions from the "start" block to the treasure.
- Place the "start" sheet on top of the sheet with the treasure.
- See if your friend can follow the instructions to the treasure.
- Do you have any debugging to do?
- Now have your friend write a code for you to follow!

start

PERSISTENCE

Things don't always turn out right the first time. It can be tempting to give up after a couple of failures. Hang in there! Persistence, or the ability to keep trying, is one of the most important skills to have if you want to think like a coder.

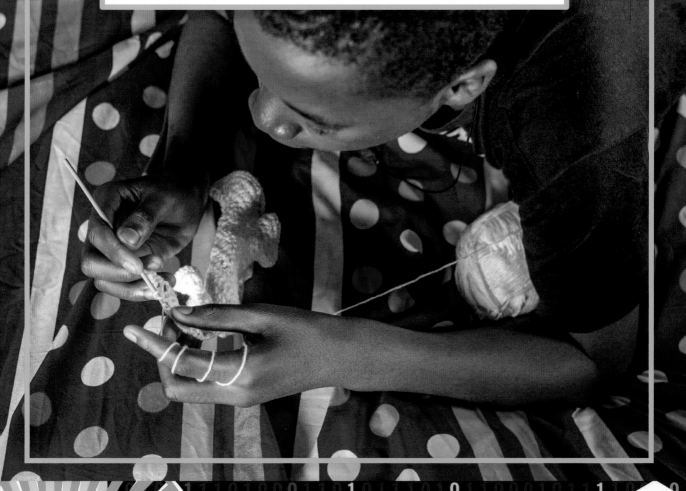

Code can include more than words and symbols. You can make a language as visual and creative as you want it to be. Talk to your friend about other elements of communication like color, temperature, and position that can also convey information.

Codes with color could be as simple as a traffic light using green for go and red for stop or as complex as flags used to communicate with ships.

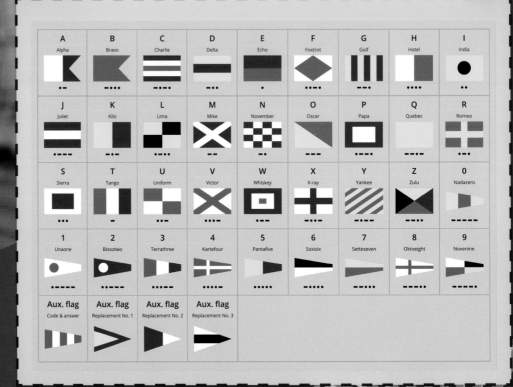

TRY IT!

Use colors to build a language for music.

- Create a language that links colors to musical actions like clapping, stomping, whistling, and humming.
- On a blank sheet of paper, draw a picture using two or three colors used in your language.
- Fold the paper in half from left to right three times.
- When you open it up, you'll have a code of eight musical actions.
- Perform your musical code with a friend!

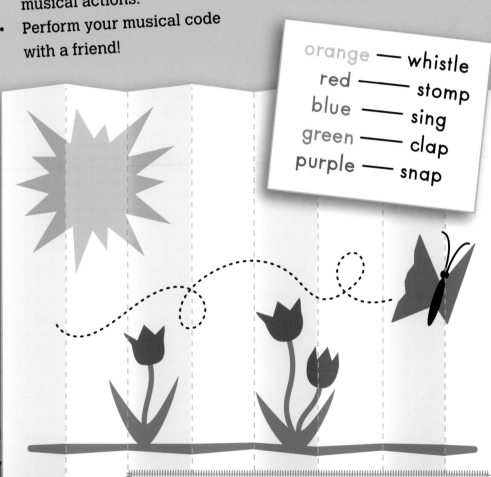

orange — whistle
red — stomp
blue — sing
green — clap
purple — snap

This drawing would make a song that goes like this:
whistle, clap / whistle, clap / whistle, stomp, clap / clap / stomp, clap / stomp, clap / sing, clap / sing, clap.

Creative Code

If you think like a coder, you can figure out instructions even when the language is new and creative. Sometimes you need to stretch your brain to see how code elements are being expressed. As code gets more creative, bugs can be harder to see. Take your time, and walk through the program to see what's working and what needs to be fixed.

GROWTH

You can get better at something with practice. When you first learn to ride a bike, you often start with training wheels. You have to work hard to be able to ride on two wheels! You can practice thinking like a coder and improve your skills too.

TRY IT!

Make a coded map only you can read!

- Invent a language that uses images to code areas of your room, the things in your room, and items that you want to hide.
- Hide an object that you will find later.
- Draw a picture that uses different images for the area of the room where you hid the item, the thing that you hid your item in, and the item itself.
- Then you have a program that acts as a map that only you can read!

KEY
cloud = center of room
rain = near the door
clear sky = by the window
swings = under the bed
merry-go-round = in dresser
seesaw = top of closet
slide = diary
fence = chocolate
bunny = markers

Using the picture and the code, you can see that the diary is under the bed in the middle of the room!

Just as recipes can use the same ingredients to make different dishes, a coding language lets you use the same instructions to make different programs. A handful of instructions can make dozens of unique programs.

TRY IT!

Cut sheets of paper into quarters, and draw symbols that stand for dance moves you like to do, one on each piece. Then arrange the papers to make a dance!

Once you've practiced the dance a few times, change the order of the papers. You've used the same symbols to create a new dance!

Each symbol has more meaning than what you see on the piece of paper. They may not seem exciting on their own, but when you put them together, you can create something amazing!

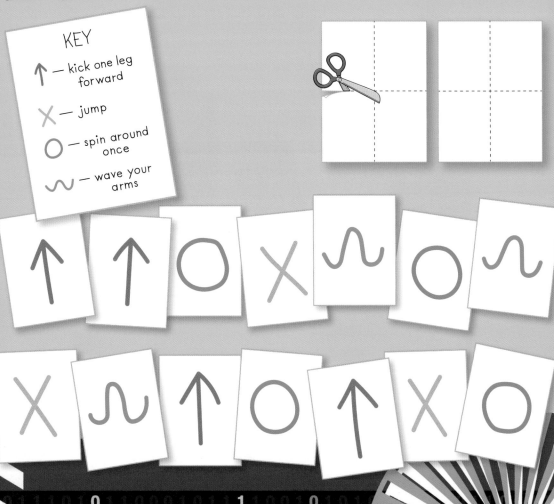

KEY

↑ — kick one leg forward

✕ — jump

○ — spin around once

∿ — wave your arms

Keep It Up

Do you enjoy thinking like a coder? Maybe you feel like trying more coding activities! As you continue recognizing patterns and dreaming up languages, don't forget the following:

- Practice makes perfect.
- When something feels tough, break it into smaller, simpler pieces.
- Keep trying when you make mistakes.
- Make small changes to improve and get where you need to be.
- Don't be scared to try something new.

Use the resources on page 31 to explore more coding concepts and activities.

CODE IT WITH COLOR!

Hex color codes use numbers and letters to tell a computer how much red, green, and blue light to mix to create colors on a computer screen. A hex color code has six numbers and letters. The first two tell the computer how much red to use, the second two are for green, and the last two are for blue. The higher the number or letter, the more of the color the computer mixes in.

This is a hex number that represents a shade of green.

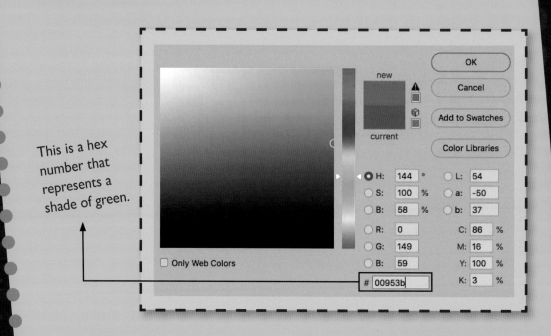

Let's take a look at some of the hex color codes inside a box of Crayola crayons!

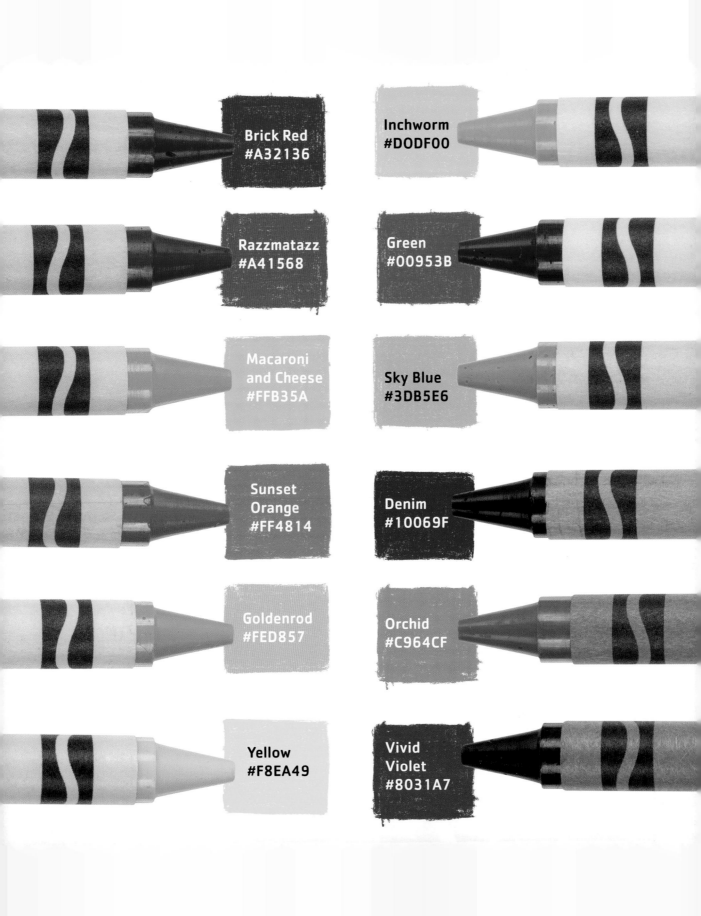

Brick Red
#A32136

Inchworm
#D0DF00

Razzmatazz
#A41568

Green
#00953B

Macaroni
and Cheese
#FFB35A

Sky Blue
#3DB5E6

Sunset
Orange
#FF4814

Denim
#10069F

Goldenrod
#FED857

Orchid
#C964CF

Yellow
#F8EA49

Vivid
Violet
#8031A7

Glossary

bug: an error in a program

code: a system of signals for communicating

debugging: finding and removing errors in a program

graphic design: using design elements such as text and images to convey information

instruction: a direction to follow

language: a system of symbols that is used to carry information

persistence: trying over and over again

sequence: the order in which something should be done

symbol: something that represents something else

visual: something that is seen

Learn More

Hour of Code Activities
https://code.org/learn

Preuitt, Sheela. *Mission Python*. Minneapolis: Lerner Publications, 2020.

Prottsman, Kiki. *How to Be a Coder*. New York: DK, 2019.

Scratch
https://scratch.mit.edu/ideas

Scrivano, Álvaro. *Coding with ScratchJr*. Minneapolis: Lerner Publications, 2019.

Index

Photo Acknowledgments

Image credits: Ongala/Shutterstock.com, p. 4; Andrey_Popov/Shutterstock.com, p. 5; Littlekidmoment/Shutterstock.com, p. 6; Wikimedia Commons (public domain), p. 7; Los Angeles County Museum of Art www.lacma.org, p. 8 (brocade); David Monniaux/Wikimedia Commons (CC BY-SA 3.0), p. 8 (loom); Laura K. Westlund/ Independent Picture Service, pp. 9, 14, 18, 21, 24, 26; Ursula Page/Shutterstock. com, p. 10; Megan Betteridge/Shutterstock.com, p. 11; myboys.me/Shutterstock. com, p. 12; Gianna Stadelmyer/Shutterstock.com, p. 13; Courtesy of the Sherborne School, p. 15 (Alan Turing); Elliott Brown/flickr (CC BY 2.0), p. 15 (code machine); SpeedKingz/Shutterstock.com, p. 16; courtesy Canva, p. 17 (top); Meehee1234/ Wikimedia Commons (CC BY-SA 4.0), p. 17 (bottom); i_am_zews/Shutterstock. com, p. 19; Askolds Berovskis/Shutterstock.com, p. 20 (traffic light); Hampus design/Shutterstock.com, p. 20 (flags); Tetra Images, LLC/Alamy Stock Photo, p. 23; Hananeko_Studio/Shutterstock.com, p. 25; Independent Picture Service, p. 28. Design elements: magic pictures/Shutterstock.com; Podursky/Shutterstock.com.

Cover: magic pictures/Shutterstock.com (computer code); Podursky/Shutterstock. com (geometric shapes).

About the Author

Kiki is a computer science educator, author, and curriculum developer. Her groundbreaking work in elementary computer science has changed the face of technology in grade schools around the world. In her spare time, she runs an educational YouTube channel, KIKIvsIT, which has helped her win multiple Innovator of the Year Awards.